Secrets to the Kingdom

Abiding

15 Discipleship Studies
Question/Answer Format
Ages 14-99

Angie Meadows

Study based on the KJV Bible version.

A Thousand Tears, LLC
PO Box 1373
Huntington, WV 25715

But seek first the kingdom of God,
and his righteousness;
and all these things
shall be added unto you.
Matthew 6:33

Table of Contents

Introduction

This is a question and answer 15-week Bible study.

- **It is in the practice of meditating on God's Word that we develop the mind of Christ.** *For "who has known the mind of the Lord that he may instruct Him? But we have the mind of Christ. 1 Corinthians 2:16*

- **It is in this practice that we may be raised above our circumstances and be seated in heavenlies with Christ Jesus.** *And raised us up together and made us sit together in heavenly places in Christ Jesus. Ephesians 2:6*

- **When we position our minds and align our hearts in the heavenly places with Christ Jesus then we are no longer controlled by the things of this world.** *If then you were raised (resurrected) with Christ, seek those things which are above, where Christ is sitting at the right hand of God. <u>Set your mind on things above</u>, not on things on the earth. Colossians 3:1-2*

- **There is a spiritual ear that must be activated.** Pride, arrogance, stubbornness and a hard heart are symptoms of a spiritually deaf ear. Humility, surrender, and dependency creates boldness to stand for truth and are signs of a spiritually awakened person. *But others fell on good ground, sprang up, and yielded a crop a hundredfold." When He had said these things He cried, "He who has ears to hear, let him hear!" Luke 8:8*

- **There are spiritually enlightened eyes** *...the eyes of your understanding being enlightened; that you may know what the hope of His calling is, what are the riches of the glory of His inheritance in the saints...Ephesians 1:18*

- **Now, Jesus prays for us to be in oneness with the Father through Christ,** *...that they may be one, as You, Father, are in Me, and I in You; that they also may be one in Us, that the world may believe that You sent Me. John 17:21*

- **Then, we are far above the principalities and powers of this world.** *...far above all principalities and power and might and dominion, and every name that is named, Ephesians 1:21*

- **Studying God's Word is the way to divide the truth from the lies and not be led astray in these last days.** *Study to show yourself approved unto God, a workman who needs not to be ashamed, rightly dividing the word of truth. 2 Timothy 2:15*

- Studying verses in the Bible gives us wisdom. We add to this study principles, memory verses, life application, a challenge and prayer prompts which will activate the ability to apply this wisdom to our life. As we pray and meditate on the Word, it will initiate a spontaneous revelation from the Holy Spirit.

- This study uses both hemispheres of the brain. The left brain is analytical and reasoning to help you identify truths in the Word of God. Then the inclusion of the right brain activity connects your spirit and soul and opens your ears to revelation knowledge and can enlighten your spiritual eyes to watch for visions and see what the Father is doing. *...Verily, verily, I say to you, the Son can do nothing of Himself, but what He sees the Father do; ... John 5:19* With these skills, you can apply what you are learning to your life and develop a strong core of identity in Christ and begin to trust yourself with solid decision-making skills.

Principles

1. Abiding in Christ is staying connected to the vine.
2. Believers do not let their hearts be troubled and are not afraid.
3. Trusting in the Lord conquers all fears.
4. To enter into God's rest is a work of believing.
5. Obedience is safety and protection.
6. A peacemaker is righteous.
7. What you compromise to keep you will lose.
8. Transformation comes with a renewed mind.
10. Death and life are in the power of the tongue.
11. Right living is the path for a healthy life.
12. Complaining and arguing is immaturity.
13. Your actions will reveal the treasures of your heart.
14. God rewards those who serve Him.
15. I am a child of God.
16. Salvation is a gift from God.

Lesson 1

Abiding in Christ

---

*I am the vine; you are the branches. If a man remains in me and
I in him, he will bear much fruit; apart from me you can do
nothing. John 15:5*

Abide means remain, continue, dwell or abiding.

1. John 15:4 What is required of us before we can bear fruit?

2. John 15:5 Will we have any lasting fruit in our lives if we are
not abiding? Why not?

3. John 15:2 Will a husbandman prune branches that are fruit
bearing?

4. John 15:1-2 Will the husbandman cut off dead branches? Why?

5. John 15:2 How can someone become likened unto a dead branch?

6. John 15:2 Can a merely professing Christian not a real Christian be cut off?

7. John 15:6 Is it necessary to abide in Christ to be fruitful?

8. John 15:7 What is a condition to having our prayers answered?

9. John 15:8 What is the purpose of bearing fruit?

10. John 15:9-14 What are the conditions of abiding? Outline verses 10-13 and tell me what it would look like to abide in His love.

Verse 10:

Verse 11:

Verse 12:

Verse 13:

11. John 15:14 What is the reward for abiding?

12. John 15:11 What is a true sign to know that we are abiding in Christ?

13. John 15:15 If we abide, what are we called? What's the blessing?

14. John 15:16 How can we be chosen?

15. John 13:35 How will others recognize we are abiding in Christ?

Principle
Abiding in Christ is staying connected to the vine.

Memory Verse

John 15:5 I am the vine; you are the branches. If a man remains in me and I in him, he will bear much fruit; apart from me you can do nothing.

Draw a picture of a vine bearing good fruit.

Application

1. What would a withered life look like?

2. What would an abiding in the vine of Christ life look like?

3. What in your life is dead and needs to be pruned? This may be a toxic emotion or something or someone that causes you mental, emotional or physical suffering. It could be an area where you just can't believe God knows what He is doing.

Write a Prayer and Confess to God how impossible it is for you to abide in Christ consistently. Ask the Lord for the faith to believe He exists and is a rewarder of those who seek Him. *But without faith it is impossible to please Him. For he that comes to God must believe that He is, and that He is a rewarder of those who diligently seek Him. Hebrews 11:6*

Challenge Take a verse and write your own question and answer.

Abiding
1. There will be lasting fruit.
2. There will be pruning.
3. Stories of answered prayers.
4. A life that glorifies God.
5. Trusting in Christ.
6. Known as a follower (disciple) of Christ.
7. Desiring to glorify God.

My Responsibility
1. Keep commandments
2. Open my heart to receive the joy of the Lord.
3. Love others.
4. Lay down my life (selfishness) and serve others.
5. Answer His call on my life to serve Him.
6. Draw near Him intentionally.

Blessings
1. I am called a friend of God.
2. My prayers are answered.
3. I will know what the Father reveals to Jesus.

Answers

1. It is required for us to abide or remain in Christ.
2. No, we will not have lasting fruit because we are only a branch. The power comes from the vine, not the branch. A cut off branch withers and dies.
3. Yes, fruit producing vines will be pruned. Pruned vines will produce more fruit the next year.
4. Yes, because they are useless. Dead vines bear no fruit.

5. They are disobedient and not repentant or yielded to Christ.

6. No, they were never part of the vine.

7. Yes. A Christian must abide, or they will wither.

8. The condition to having prayers answered is to be abiding or trusting in Christ.

9. The purpose of bearing fruit is to glorify God. So, they will see your good works and glorify your father in heaven. Matthew 5:16 We will also be known as His disciples.

10. I must continue in His love to bear fruit. Verse 10 Keep commandments; Verse 11 Complete joy; Verse12 Love one-another; Verse 13 Lay down your life in service for others; Verse 14 Keep His commandments.

11. We are Jesus's friends.

12. A true sign that I am abiding is that I have joy. I naturally smile and are generally content.

13. This verse calls us friends of Christ. We are blessed to know what the Father has revealed to Jesus.

14. God chooses us. We are appointed to go and bear fruit. James 4:8 Draw close to God, and He will draw close to us. John 3:16 Whosoever will…. We must receive the call on our life and come to God. We have personal responsibility to mature as a believer.

15. We will be recognized by our love for one another.

May your spiritual ear be opened to hear the call of God.

Lesson 2

New Nature

Peace, I leave with you; my peace I give you. I do not give to you as the world gives. Do not let your hearts be troubled and do not be afraid. John 14:27

Peace-A state of quiet or tranquility; freedom from disturbance or agitation. Harmony. Accord.

1. James 1:25 How will we know when the Word of God is truly coming alive in our hearts?

2. James 1:26 How do we know we are out of step with God?

3. Romans 8:11 Can we have assurance that we will be resurrected like Christ?

4. Romans 13:14 What can we do to keep ourselves from sinning?

5. Hebrews 5:11 What is a characteristic of spiritual immaturity?

6. Hebrews 5:14 What is characteristic of spiritual maturity?

7. Hebrews 6:10 Is God forgetful of what you have done for Him?

8. Hebrews 6:12 What will we, who follow Christ, inherit?

9. Romans 2:7 What two things does God expect us to do?

10. Ephesians 2:10 Why were we created?

11. John 10:28-29 Can we have assurance of salvation?

12. 1 John 3:20 What if I don't feel saved?

13. 1 John 4:4 Can I overcome the world?

14. 1 Peter 4:1-2 What are the two purposes of suffering in the flesh?

15. John 15:26 What will the Father send us?

16. John 14:26 Who is our helper and what will He do?

Principle
Believers do not let their hearts be troubled and are not afraid.

Memory Verse

*Peace, I leave with you; my peace I give you. I
do not give to you as the world gives. Do not let
your hearts be troubled and do not be afraid.*
John 14:27

Draw a dove with a ribbon of peace to your heart to receive a
blessing.

Application

1. What do you think it would look like to "remain" in His love today?

2. What would it look like to clothe yourself in Christ?

3. Abiding in Christ is not rules or legalism, but it does start with the discipline to pray, read the Word, and ask the Holy Spirit to teach you to seek Him. Talk to the Lord about your struggles to mature and grow spiritually. Confess any complacency.

Write your own Prayer like this: Lord, give me your peace, help my heart not to be troubled or afraid. If I am troubled, help me to recognize it and please have the Holy Spirit remind me of your Words. Strengthen me to remain in your love. In Jesus name, Amen **John 14:26-27; 15:10**

Challenge: The Word is living. Learn to pray the living Word and this will infuse life into your Spirit. *In the beginning was the Word, and the Word was with God, and the Word was God. And the Word was made flesh and dwelt among us… John 1:1,14 For the Word of God is living… Hebrews 4:12*

God's Work
• God doesn't forget the good we have done.
• God keeps us and no man can pluck us out of His hand.
• God is greater than our condemning hearts.

Holy Spirit's Work
1. Quicken our moral bodies
2. Be our helper.
3. Be our Comforter.
4. Be our teacher.
5. Remind us of what we have learned.
Holy Spirit is also called the Spirit of Truth and He leads to the perfect Law of Liberty.

Our Work
1. Clothe yourself in Christ.
2. Train yourself to discern good and evil.
3. Develop patience and consistency to do good and wait for promises.
4. Seek glory, honor and immortality
5. Respond to suffering with the mind of Christ and cease to sin.
6. A hearer and doer of the Word.

Two Signs of Immaturity
1. Immature speech
2. Dull of Hearing

Answers

1. We will start look at the Law of Liberty (freedom not to sin) and be a doer of the Word and not just a hearer.

2. Our speech will show the intentions of our heart.
3. Yes, because God's Word says His Spirit will quicken us and raise our mortal bodies.
4. Do not think about how to gratify the desires of the flesh; instead, clothe yourself in Christ.
5. Spiritual immaturity is dull of hearing and usually struggle to hear truth or receive correction.
6. You train yourself consistently to distinguish between good and evil.
7. No, God will not forget what you have done for Him.
8. We will inherit the promises through faith and patience if we are not slothful.
9. He expects us to patiently and consistently do good and to seek for glory, honor and immortality.
10. We were created for good works.
11. Yes, no man can take us out of the Father's hand.
12. God is greater than our heart. Stand on God's Word, not on fickle emotions that will always end land us in condemnation.
13. Yes, because greater is He that is in you, than he that is in the world.
14. Suffering causes us to be done with sin and eagerly follow God if we develop the same mind Christ had with His suffering.
15. The Father will send us the Spirit of truth, the Comforter (Holy Spirit).
16. The advocate is the Holy Spirit and He will teach us all things and remind us of what Jesus said to us. *This is why it is important to know the Word, so the Holy Spirit can remind us of it.

May the Word of God flow in your heart and from your lips.

Lesson 3

TRUST

Trust-to place confidence in; to rely on.

1. Job 13:15 How much did Job trust in God?

2. Psalm 25:1-2 Who does David trust with his fears and what two things does he pray?

3. Psalm 31:6 Who does David not trust? Who does David trust?

4. Psalm 37:3 What two things do we need to do? What is the promise?

5. Psalm 40:3 What can we ask for in times of trouble to help others trust the Lord?

6. Psalm 56:3 What should I do when I am afraid?

7. Psalm 62:8 Who is our refuge that we can trust? Who can we tell all our secrets?

8. Psalm 115:9 Who is our help and shield?

9. Psalm 118:8 What is better than confidence in a person?

10. Psalm 143:8 Again David lifts up his soul to God. What two things is David praying?

11. Psalm 144:2 What five ways does David use to describe God?

12. Proverbs 3:5 How much should we trust God? Will trusting God make any sense?

13. Proverbs 28:26 How can I tell if I am being foolish? In verse 25, what kind of heart will make strife?

14. Nahum 1:7 Who is our protector in the day of trouble? Who does the Lord personally know?

15. Matthew 27:46 Will God always deliver us the way we think he should?

16. Luke 18:9-14 What did the man do who trusted in himself?

Principle

Trusting in the Lord conquers all fears.

Memory Verses

When I am afraid, I put my trust in you. Psalm 56:3

Write out Psalm 56:3:

Application

1. Listen to your speech. *For out of the abundance of the heart the mouth speaks. Matthew 12:34* Do you praise yourself? Do you speak of helplessness? Are you struggling with anger or bitterness?

2. The Psalmist David ran for his life for years and turned every trouble into a triumph by lifting his soul (which is his emotions) to God and exchanging them for trust. Lift your soul up to God here and give him your troubles.

3. Find one friend who is anxious/fearful and coach them on how to trust God.

Write a Prayer Confess your fears to the Lord and ask Him to give you the ability to trust in Him.

Challenge Intentionally recognize physical signals of anxiety, stress or worry and exchange them to trust in the Lord. Do it like this when you feel anxious: "Lord, I have forgotten to trust you, forgive me and help me to trust you more. I need you now Lord."

Characteristics of Trust
1. Lift up my soul to God.
2. Trust in God and not in my own strength.
3. Be resolved to trust God no matter what! "Though He slay me, yet I will trust in God." Job 13:15

Prayers of the Psalmist
1. Cause me to walk in your ways.
2. Protect me in the day of trouble.
3. Help me exchange fear for trust.
4. Give me a new song
5. Let me not be ashamed.

Characteristics of God
• Protector
• Deliverer
• Loving-Kindness (Goodness)

• Stronghold (High Tower)
• Shield
• Helper
• Refuge
• Fortress

Promise
Dwell in the land and be fed!

Answers

1. Job trusted God with his very life.

2. David lifts his soul to God.

David asks God to not let him be ashamed.

David asks God to not let his enemies' triumph over him.

3. David doesn't trust those with lying lips. David trusts God.

4. We are to trust in the Lord and do good. The promise is that we shall dwell in the land and be fed.

5. We can ask God to give us a new song of praise.

6. What time we are afraid, we should trust in God.

7. God is our refuge. God can be trusted with the secrets of our heart.

8. God is our helper and our shield to protect me.

9. It is better to trust in the Lord than in a person. Trust in the Lord (center verse of the Bible)

10. A. Let me hear your loving-kindness in the morning.

B. Cause me to know your way that I should walk.

11. 1) Loving-kindness (goodness)

2) Fortress

3) Stronghold (high tower)

4) Deliverer

5) Shield

12. We are to trust in the Lord with all our hearts. No, it will not make sense, he says to "lean not" to our own understanding.

13. A foolish person trusts in themselves. A greedy, proud person will cause strife.

14. The Lord is our protector in the day of trouble. The Lord personally knows those that trust in Him.

15. God doesn't usually deliver us the way we anticipate He will. Jesus was not delivered from suffering but from eternal death. His suffering was for a higher purpose. His suffering conquered death. Read Isaiah 55:9 *For as the heavens are higher than the earth, so are my ways higher than your ways, and my thoughts than your thoughts.*

16. A person who trust in themselves will despise others and puff themselves up with self-adoration rehearsing their good deeds.

May you step into the kingdom of heaven as you learn to trust in God.

Lesson 4

RESTING

For he that is entered into his rest, he also has ceased from his own works, as God did from His. Hebrews 4:10

Rest- is a peace of mind and spirit; free from anxiety and disturbance; to remain confident and trusting.

1.Hebrews 3:15 What two things should we do today?

2. Hebrews 3:16 When some heard God's voice what did they do?

3. Hebrews 3:17 A) With whom was God angry (grieved)?

B) What was their sin?

C) What caused a hard heart?

4. Hebrews 3:18 If we are anxious, what should we look for in our heart?

5. Hebrews 3:19 Again, what will keep us from entering His rest?

6. Hebrews 4:1 What is our promise?

7. Hebrews 4:2 What does the Word need to be mixed with for us to profit from it?

8. Hebrews 4:3 A) If we believe, what is our earthly reward?

B) How long ago did God prepare for us to enter His rest?

9. Hebrews 4:4 A) What did God do on the seventh day?

B) Why do you think God rested?

10. Hebrews 4:6 A) Does preaching (hearing the good news) bring us into rest?

B) What keeps us from entering God's rest?

11. Hebrews 4:7 What are the two commands?

12. Hebrews 4:10 How do you know when you have entered His rest?

13. Hebrews 4:11 A) What should we make every effort to do?

B) What is the opposite of resting in Christ?

14. Hebrews 4:12 A) What will conquer our unbelief?

B) How is the Word of God described?

15. Hebrews 4:13 Is there anything hidden from God?

16. Hebrews 4:14-16 A) **Jesus is our High Priest.** He sympathizes with our weaknesses. So, what should we do?

B) What should we ask for at the throne of grace?

Principle
To enter into God's rest is a work of believing.

Memory Verse

For he that is entered into his rest, he also has ceased from his own works, as God did from His. Hebrews 4:10

Application

1. Whose responsibility is it to keep my heart soft and tender towards God?

2. The greatest sin of the Israelites in the wilderness was <u>unbelief</u>. If I want God's rest (peace) this is work. It is work to enter into a place of rest.
   First, I must intentionally stop the grumbling and complaining.
   Secondly, I must stop agreeing with and rehearsing my fears.
   Then, I need to resist fear and take dominion over my thought life with prayer and the word of God.
   Lastly, I must realize that anxiety is doing my own work and release my cares to God.
   Which one do you need to do most today?

3. Intentionally cultivate a quiet heart today. Discharge any anxiety as you write these words, "I trust you Lord, help me to trust you more."

Write a Prayer Ask the Lord to help you disconnect from the suffering of feeling and re-feeling your fears and **receive** His gift of faith.

Challenge If I am anxious and not emotionally resting, I am doing my own work. My anxiety is a signal to stop and give the thing I am stressing over to God. Set your intention today to "rest" and reset with a deep breath ten times throughout your day.

Root causes of Unbelief
• fear
• anger
• bitterness
• depression
• sadness
• confusion
• anxiety
• double mindedness
• stubbornness

Characteristics of Unbelief
1. Grumbling
2. Complaining
3. Refusal to believe
4. Dull of hearing
5. Hard heart refusal to mature

Developing Skills of a Resting Heart
• confidence
• trusting God with uncertainty
• steadfast
• believing
• contentment

Characteristics of a Believing Heart
1. Joy
2. Patience
3. Kindness
4. Repenting often
5. Gentle
6. Teachable

Answers

1. Hear His voice and do not harden our hearts.

2. When they heard God's voice they rebelled or became provoked.

3. A) Those who sinned.

B) Hard heart (disobedience).

C) Unbelief

4. We should look for our unbelief.

5. Our unbelief will keep us in disobedience wandering in a wilderness. This will be exhibited by grumbling, complaining and discontentment.

6. The Promise is rest.

7. The Word needs to be mixed with faith.

8. A) If we believe we will enter into God's rest (peace).

B) Rest was prepared for us from the foundation of the earth.

9. A) God rested on the seventh day.

B) God did not because He was tired, but as an example to us.

10. A) No, we need faith to go along with preaching or it will sound foolish. I Corinthians 1:22-29

B) A hardened heart will keep us in disobedience, and we will not be able to enter into God's rest.

11. The two instructions are to hear His voice and do not harden your heart.

12. You will stop doing your own works.

13. A) We should labor to enter His rest. This is work.
B) The opposite of resting is anxiety or fears.
14. A) Word of God rehearsed in my heart will conquer unbelief.
B) It is described as a living and sword. *Living and active (quick and powerful) sharper than a double-edged sword, penetrating (piercing) and dividing the soul and spirit, joints, and marrow. It is judges (discerns) thoughts and the attitude (intent-motive) of the heart. Hebrews 4:12*
15. No, nothing is hidden from God.
16. A) We are to come confidently (boldly) to the throne of grace.
B) We are to ask for mercy and grace.

May you believe and enter into a place of continual rest.

Lesson 5

Obedience

Obedience-an act of obeying. Think voluntary action or under authority, submissive. Obedience hears intelligently and consents with contentment. Obedience listens carefully and conforms to a command. The alternative to obedience is rebellion which ushers in tyranny which is harsh and oppressive authority.

1. John 14:15 If we love Jesus, will we obey Him?

2. John 14:16-17 What is the blessing of obedience?

3. Ephesians 6:1 A) What is the command?

B) Ephesians 6:2 What is the principle?

C) Ephesians 6:3 What are the two promises?

4. A) 1 Peter 2:13-14 To whom do we submit?

B) 1 Peter 2:14 What is the purpose of this authority?

5. Romans 13:1 A) Who establishes our authorities?

B) Romans 13:2 So, if we rebel against authority, what may happen to us?

6. Acts 5:29 When asked to do wrong what did Peter and the other apostles say?

7. 1 Peter 5:5 What character trait do we need to develop obedience?

8. 2 Timothy 2:15 How can we correctly handle the Word of God?

9. John 14:21 To whom does Christ reveal Himself?

10. John 10:27 If we follow Christ, will we know right from wrong?

11. John 10:28 A) What is our reward for following Jesus?

B) John 10:29 Can anyone snatch us out of the Father's hand?

12. A) 1 Samuel 15:22 "To obey is better than_____."

B) 1 Samuel 15:23 "Rebellion is like_____."
Arrogance (stubbornness) is like_____."

Principle
Obedience is safety and protection.

Memory Verses
Behold, to obey is better than sacrifice. 1 Samuel 15:22b

Application
1. Obedience is to do what is right. Make decisions based upon what is moral, ethical, and principle based. Obedience means to not violate our conscience and join in with rebels or cause unnecessary trouble. Is there any place in your life you are grumbling about? What should you do differently?

2. Obedience is safety. It is a word of protection not restriction. If I have a loved little pet dog, I will walk him on a leash or have a fenced in yard for his protection. Do you see obedience as protection or restriction?

3. Obedience is security. Authorities are our pillars of structure, stability, and peace in our land. Often, the person in charge doesn't deserve our respect. Therefore, instead, respect their office of authority. What authority do you resist the most?

Prayer Listening is a maturity skill, and we need an ear tuned to hear His voice. This spiritually tuned ear is a gift. Pray for the gift of a spiritual hearing.

Challenge Today clothe yourself in humility (gentleness). Reset 3-4 times throughout the day. Honoring our authority is separate from obedience and is intentional. This means we obey with a happy heart and without grumbling and complaining. <u>Honor your authorities not only with obedience but with a smile.</u>

Principles
• Obedience: gives us the power to overcome the world. 1 John 5:4 *The secret is to be born of God.
• Rebellion brings us into judgment. Romans 13:2
• Honoring our parents is our duty. Ephesians 6:1-2

Life Skills
• Clothe ourselves in humility. 1 Peter 5:5
• Submit to authorities. 1 Peter 2:13-14
• Studying God's Word carefully. 2 Timothy 2:15
• Listening carefully for the voice of your shepherd. John 10:27

Promises
1. All will go well with you. Ephesians 6:1-3
2. You will live a long life. Ephesians 6:1-3
3. Eternal Life John 10:28
4. We will have the Comforter, Counselor, Spirit of Truth John 14:16-17

Answers

1. Yes, if we love the Lord, we will obey to the best of our understanding.

2. He will give us a counselor—Spirit of Truth through His presence within us.

3. A. The command is to obey your parents.

B. The principle is to honor your father and mother.

C. The promise is that it will go well, and you will have a long life.

4. A) We submit to every governing institution because authority comes from God: governors, police officers, teachers, employers, parents, ministers.

B) The purpose of authority is to punish those who do evil and commend those who do well.

5. A) It is God who establishes authority.

B) Judgment is brought on us when we choose to rebel.

6. We should obey God rather than men!

7. The character skill we need is humility. We are to be clothed in humility.

8. Study the Word of God so you can rightly handle the Word of God.

9. Christ shows Himself to those who love and obey His commands.

10. Yes, My sheep will hear My voice and follow Me.

11. A) Our reward is eternal life.

B) No, no one can snatch you out of the hand of the Lord.

12. A) To obey is better than sacrifice.

B) Rebellion is like witchcraft or the sin of divination. Arrogance (stubbornness) is like idolatry.

May you have a heart that loves big.

.

Lesson 6
Friends

Perverse-means improper, incorrect, corrupt, obstinate, cranky, hardheaded.

1. Proverbs 13:20 What happens if I have a companion that is wise vs. one that is foolish?

2. Proverbs 17:17a What is the characteristics of a friend?

3. Proverbs 27:6 What kind of wounds might you receive from a good friend?

4. Proverbs 27:17 What do friends do for each other?

5. Proverbs 17:9 What does it mean to cover a transgression?

6. Proverbs 16:28 What kind of a person is not a good friend?

7. Proverbs 22:24-25 What kind of a person would not make a good friend? What does it mean to be ensnared?

8. Proverbs 28:24 What makes us a companion (friend) of a destroyer?

9. Matthew 26:48-49 Why might a pretend friend kiss you?

10. John 13:34 What is the commandment?

11. John 14:21 How can we be friends with Jesus?

12. John 15:13 How do you know a person has "great love" for you?

13. John 15:15 What evidence do we have that we are a friend of Jesus?

14. 1 Corinthians 15:33 What corrupts good manners?

15. James 4:4 What would disqualify us from being a friend of God?

16. James 2:23 What did Abraham do to become a friend of God?

*Check out James 3:13-18 and list characteristics of the friend of the world vs. friend of God.

Friend Contrast: Worldly vs. Spiritual	
Worldly =unspiritual and from the devil	**God= wise and understanding**
• Harboring bitter envy	• Humble; Meek
• Selfish ambition	• Pure
• Boasting	• Peace-loving
• Denying the truth	• Considerate
• Disorder	• Submissive
• Evil practices	• Full of mercy
• Sensual	• Bearing good fruit
	• Impartial
	• Sincere
Confusion is a signal we are aligned in some way with worldly thinking. A **harvest of peace** is aligned with wisdom.	

Principle
A peacemaker is righteous.

Memory Verse
Peacemakers who sow in peace raise a harvest of righteousness.
James 3:18

Application

1. You must earn the right to speak into someone's life.
Ask yourself is it any of my business? Are they under my authority? Are they asking for my help? Are they giving me permission to speak into their lives? Have I corrected myself first? Then I can be iron that sharpens iron in a friendship. Who sharpens you?

2. Untangle yourself gently from a hot-tempered person.
Tolerating an angry person, may mean that I need to shrink to be invisible. Or I may learn their ways and become addicted to abusing others with my own anger. Is there anyone in your life that is angry and who needs distance from your heart?

3. Selfish self vs sanctified self.
A selfish person is always out for gain. They care more for themselves and demand their own ways and throw fits when they don't get it. Frequently, they externalize all their internal chaos on people near them.
A sanctified self will leave an intolerable person for the reasons of self-preservation. They may go in and out of relationships quickly, but their heart will not be safe enough to be carefree in the presence of a selfish person.
A true friendship is carefree, and our hearts will be safe to be our authentic self. Do you have an authentic friend like this?

Write a Prayer and ask the Lord for a strong friend to mentor you and for a friend you can mentor.

Challenge Make people earn the right to be your friend. Do not share your inner most secrets with just anyone. Choose 1-3 close friends to be in your inner circle. Keep your circle small. Who keeps showing up for you?

Answers
1. A wise companion will make me wiser; but a companion with fools will bring me destruction.
2. A true friend always loves.
3. A good friend would tell you the truth and give you correction.

4. Good friends sharpen each other to become stronger and wiser.
5. To cover a transgression or a wrong done means I don't repeat the matter to others.
6. A forward/perverse (stubborn, hard-headed) person would not make a good friend.
7. Don't make friends with a hot-tempered (Angry, furious) person. Ensnared means I will be trapped.
8. Robbing our family or exploiting them or embezzling money under false pretenses makes us a companion to the destroyer.
9. A false friend that uses kind words or a kiss for selfish motives is a betrayer.
10. The commandment is love one another as Jesus loves us.
11. When we obey Christ's commands, we are friends and not servants.
12. Laying down my own life means I am not selfish but have great love. A parent is called to lay down their life (needs) for their infant's care.
13. Jesus has made known to us things He has heard from the Father. When we study God's Word, we will consistently grow and mature.
14. Bad company with evil communication will corrupt my good manners.
15. Being a friend of the world will make me an enemy of God. I must choose sides and get off the fence.
16. Abraham just believed. This qualified him to be a friend of God.

May you have a friend who sticks closer than a brother.

Lesson 7

Combatting Substance Abuse

In the end it bites like a snake and poisons like a viper. Proverbs 23:32

Self-control is restraint exercised over one's own impulses, emotions or desires.

1. Proverbs 4:17,19 Alcohol is associated with what behavior?

2. Proverbs 13:20 Who should be our close friends/companions?

3.Proverbs 21:17 What will alcohol rob from us?

4.Proverbs 23:31 How do we stay away from alcohol?

5.Proverbs 23:29 What does alcohol (wine, beer, liquor) give us?

6. Proverbs 31:3-5 What are the instructions in these verses?

7. Romans 12:1-2 How do we stay away from other harmful substances?

8. Romans 13:14 How can we resist temptations?

9. 1 Corinthians 10:23 What does Paul say about substances that can control us?

10. 1 Corinthians 10:21 Can we sit the fence and partake of Holy things one day and worldly things the next day?

11. 1 Corinthians 15:33; Proverbs 13:20 Can we have close companions with those who are fools?

12. Revelations 3:16 Can we be only partially sold out to Christ?

13. Matthew 6:22-23 Describe healthy and unhealthy eyes?

14. Matthew 13:12 If we reject truth what happens to us?

Principles
What you compromise to keep you will lose.

Memory Verse

In the end it bites like a snake and poisons like a
viper. Proverbs 23:32

Application
1. Any substances like alcohol or mind-altering drugs will make us vulnerable to violence or being in the wrong place at the wrong time. Are there any peers that are leading you down the wrong path that you need to distance yourself from?

2. Confusion vs. Peace *...for God is not the author of confusion, but of peace... 1 Corinthians 14:33* If there is confusion in any area of your life, pray about that area and ask God for His wisdom. *If any of you lack wisdom, let him ask of God, who gives to all generously and without finding fault, and it shall be given. James 1:5* Ask for wisdom here:

3. God's ways are considered foolish to the wise. *For the foolishness of God is wiser than men, and the weakness of God is strong than men...but God has chosen the foolish things of the world to confound the wise, and God has chosen the weak things of the world to confound the things which are mighty...1 Corinthians 1:25, 27.* What things does Scripture teach that seem utterly foolish to you?

Write a Prayer and ask God for a steadfast heart to follow Him even when others may mock you. *They (God's people) will have no fear of evil tidings (bad news); their hearts are fixed (steadfast), trusting in the Lord. Psalm 112:7*

Challenge Build the character skills to intentionally be self-controlled.

Choose an area of your life to develop a good habit.

Disciplines	
Make your bed every morning.	
Do your dishes every night.	
Clean your house entirely once a week.	
Clean your closets once a month.	
Limit game or tv time to a few hours a week.	
Eat 5-10 fruits and vegetables a day.	

Choose an area of your life to develop a healthy spiritual habit.

More Disciplines	
•	Renewing your mind.
•	Developing healthy eyes –spiritual insight
•	Understanding limitation and vulnerabilities
•	Overcoming lukewarm/complacency
•	Seeking wise companions
•	Read your Bible everyday.
•	Pray every evening.

Answers

1. Alcohol is associated with violence and makes your path dark where you make poor decisions.
2. We should be friends with wise people who make good decisions in life.

3. Alcohol will rob us of our wealth. It can destroy our productivity.
4. Don't even look at it! Change your thoughts, refute lies, breakdown strongholds. Go home a different way. Don't go down that isle at the store. Alcohol can be a serious temptation and a compromise and destroy your life.
5. It gives us sorrow, contentions, babbling, wounds without cause and woe, sorrow, strife, complaints, needless bruises, and bloodshot eyes.
6. Wine and beer are not for Kings or rulers, drinking can make a person forget their duties. It can dull our senses and limit our judgment.
7. We can present our bodies as living sacrifice: pure, holy, acceptable. Do not be conformed to this world but transformed by the renewing of your mind.
8. Clothe yourself with the Lord Jesus Christ and don't think about gratifying the desires of the flesh.
9. Do not do anything that isn't constructive and beneficial, even if it is permissible.
10. No, we cannot be fence-sitters and follow evil one day and good the next.
11. No, bad company corrupts good manners, and a companion of fools will be destroyed.
12. No, lukewarm or complacent individuals will receive chastisement.
13. Healthy eyes indicate a man with spiritual insight and eyes which are enlightened and firmly fixed on Christ. Unhealthy eyes indicate darkness, clouded judgment and serving the flesh.
14. A person that has truth and accepts it gets more truth and a person that refuses truth gets it taken away and darkness comes in.

May you dwell in the Kingdom of Heaven.

Lesson 8

Standing Alone

Do not conform any longer to the pattern of this world but be transformed by the renewing of your mind. Romans 12:2

Renewed-made new again, re-established, revived, regenerated.

1. Romans 12:1-2 How do we see things from God's point of view?

2. Romans 8:13 How do we become obedient to the promptings of the Holy Spirit so we can apply God's truth to our daily living?

3. Romans 6:4 How can we know that a person has identified with Christ's death, burial, and resurrection?

4. Romans 6:6 How do we resist sin?

5. Romans 6:13 If we truly surrender our life to Christ where should we YIELD the members of our bodies?

6. Romans 6:22 If we are servants of obedience what two things do we receive?

7. Romans 6:23 If we are servants of sin, what pay do we receive?

8. Matthew 28:20 Does God ever leave us?

9. John 14:21 Jesus says if we love him, we will do what?

10. James 4:4 How do you know if a person is an enemy of God?

11. James 4:6 Who receives the grace of God?

12. James 4:7 How do we resist the devil?

13. James 4:8 When will God come near us?

14. Daniel 1:8 How did Daniel stand-alone against a foreign pagan culture?

Principles
Transformation comes with a renewed mind.

Memory Verse

Do not conform any longer to the pattern of this world but be transformed by the renewing of your mind. Romans 12:2

Application

1. We can't possibly stand-alone until we cleanse our hands of sin and purify our hearts from being double minded. I hear my doublemindedness when I am rationalizing my poor behaviors, my sin or judging myself according to the world's standards. Where do you need help to stand strong?

2. In what practical way will you prepare to stand strong and stand alone so you won't be defiled by the world? *The prudent man sees the evil and hides himself... Proverbs 22:3*

3. The rewards of righteousness are peace. Take any part of your day that is chaotic and pray over it and ask God how to structure it to bring the fruit of peace.

Write a Prayer and ask the Lord for the gift of a transformed life. Confess any feelings of helplessness.

Challenge Think on the hard stuff 15 minutes twice a day and then let it go and renew the mind through disciplining your thought life. It is meditating on God's thoughts. It is learning to preach truth to myself and not indulge fickle emotions. What thoughts do you repetitively think that do not serve you well?

Answers

1. We become living sacrifices and refuse to conform to the world but are transformed by renewing our minds.
2. We are to live by the Spirit of God and mortify (kill) the deeds of the flesh.
3. A resurrected life walks in newness of life.
4. The old person is crucified (put to death) so we don't serve sin.
5. We are to yield our bodies to righteousness.
6. We will have fruit of holiness and everlasting life.
7. The wage of sin is death.
8. No, the LORD is with us always.
9. If we love Him, we will keep His <u>commandments</u>.
10. An enemy of God is a friend to the world.
11. God gives grace to the humble.
12. We actively resist the devil by submitting to God
13. The Lord will be near when we draw near to him. Drawing near to the Lord will help us cleanse our hands and purify our hearts.
14. Daniel purposed in his heart that he would not defile himself.

How to Stand Alone	
1.	Become a living sacrifice.
2.	Don't be conformed to the world.
3.	Be transformed by renewing your mind.
4.	Live by the Spirit.
5.	Mortify the deeds of the flesh.
6.	Walk in newness of life.
7.	Crucify the old man.
8.	Don't serve sin.
9.	Yield your body to righteousness.
10.	Obey commandments.
11.	Resist the devil.
12.	Submit to God.
13.	Draw near to God.
14.	Cleanse your hands.
15.	Purify your heart.
16.	Purpose not to defile yourself.

REWARDS
• Fruit of holiness
• Everlasting life
• Peace
• Grace

May you conquer the flesh and walk in the Spirit..

Lesson 9

DISCIPLINING THE TONGUE

Death and life are in the power of the tongue, and they that love it shall eat the fruit thereof. Proverbs 18:21

Wholesome tongue-promoting health and a peaceful mind.

1. Proverbs 18:21 What are the two kinds of words in this verse?

2. 1 Corinthians 15:33 What would corrupt good manners?

3. Proverbs 13:10 To remove strife from our homes what two things should I do?

4. 1 John 1:9 What should we do often?

5. Proverbs 15:4 What bad habit should we break?

6. Proverbs 31:26 What should be the law of our tongue?

7. Matthew 5:22 What is the rule in this verse?

8. 2 Corinthians 10:12 If we compare ourselves with others are we wise?

9. Proverbs 18:13 Should I interrupt and answer before I hear it all?

10. Titus 2:9 What's the rule?

11. Proverbs 25:28 What character skill needs to be developed in this verse?

12. Proverbs 10:12 What covers a multitude of sins?

13. Proverbs 13:1 Should we allow teasing and mocking among peers?

14. Proverbs 15:1 How should we answer someone who is harsh with us?

Principles
Death and life are in the power of the tongue.

Memory Verse

Death and life are in the power of the tongue,
and they that love it shall eat the fruit thereof.
Proverbs 18:21

Application

1. Living with the Holy Spirit inside of us we can be renewed day by day through the power of the Holy Spirit. 2 Cor. 4:16; Eph. 4:23; Col. 3:10; Gal. 2:20. Therefore, we must rely heavily on Scripture to teach and train us how to walk in the Spirit. As we model this before others, more will be caught than taught. *All Scripture is given by inspiration of God and is profitable for doctrine, for reproof, for correction, for instruction in righteousness. 2 Timothy 3:16* Are you humble enough to allow Scripture to correct you?

2. Correcting ourselves with Scripture is powerful. We can't correct others until we correct ourselves and are accountable to God to speak correctly. Proverbs 22:6 and you must train children even if it isn't pleasant. But how could we use untrained lips to train others?

3. Teaching self-control is a life-long discipline in words, emotions, actions, etc. Where do you need self-control?

Write a Prayer and ask God to give you the desire to discipline your tongue. *No discipline seems pleasant at the time, but painful. Later on, however, it produces a <u>harvest of righteousness and peace</u> for those who have been trained by it. Hebrews 12:11*

Challenge Be quick to listen and slow to speak. This takes practice. Often, we would place a piece of scotch tape on our mouth for an hour a day and not be able to speak without quoting this verse first and then taking a deep breath before we spoke to think carefully about our words. This was great training. We became patient with our speech and didn't interrupt each other. ...
let every person be swift to hear, slow to speak, slow to wrath.
James 1:19

Disciplining the Tongue
1. Ask ourselves will these words bring life or death.
2. Examine the fruit. Is it righteous?
3. Model for others how to be humble and ask for advice.
4. Confess often.
5. Break bad habits.
6. Law of our tongue is kindness.
7. No name calling.
8. No comparing.
9. No interrupting.
10. No back talking.
11. No indulging anger. Practice self-control.
12. No tattling.
13. No teasing or mocking.
14. Answer gently.

Answers

1. There are words that bring life and words that bring death.
2. Evil friends will corrupt us and ruin our good manners.
3. We are to humble ourselves and ask for advice.
4. We should confess our sins often.
5. An unwholesome tongue is a breach in our spirit. We must correct our speech in order to heal.
6. The law of our tongue is kindness. Think kind, patient, but firm as a rule.
7. The rule from this verse would be "No name calling".
8. Comparing ourselves with others is not wise.
9. The rule is no answering or interrupting until you have heard the matter.
10. There is to be no back talking. Respectful problem solving, yes, but not back talking or disrespect to authority.
11. The character skill that needs developed is self-control.
12. Love covers sin.
13. No, teasing is allowed if it is hurtful, and no mocking is to be tolerated.
14. We should answer angry people with gentleness. This calm spirit will diffuse the situation and not escalate it.

May your tongue be a tree of life.

Lesson 10

RIGHTEOUS TONGUE

Righteousness-purity of the heart, justice, honesty, and virtue.

1. What behaviors accompany lying? Proverbs 6:17-19

2. What is the secret to hate a forward mouth? Proverbs 8:13

3. What should we pray for so we will know what is acceptable? Proverbs 10:32

4. What will be established forever; what will only last for a moment? Proverbs 12:19

5. Idle chatter leads to what? Proverbs 14:23

6. What are an ungodly person's lips like? Prov. 16:27

7. If we lie to someone, what does it show about how we feel about them? Proverbs 26:28

8. Who did David complain to? Psalm 55:1-5

9. What did God promise David? Psalm 55:22

10. If we have a deceitful tongue, what should we do? Psalm 120:2

11. What is the speech of a violent person? Psalm 140:1-3

12. What does David pray about an evil speaker? Psalm 140:8-11

13. How do we stop lying? Ephesians 4:22-25

14. How can we know if our communications are corrupt?
Ephesians 4:29

15. Should we curse, tease, be rude or talk foolishly with others?
Ephesians 5:4

16. How do we stop filthiness and foolish talk? Ephesians 5:4

17. The damage our speech can do is likened unto what? James 3:5-6

18. What can defile your whole body? James 3:6

Principles
Right living is the path for a healthy life.

Memory Verse

In the way of righteousness is life, and in the pathway thereof there is no death. Proverbs 12:28

Application

1. Lying, deceiving others, and selfishness causes a person not to be able to love another. Break selfishness by doing an act of kindness towards others, denying self and sacrificing time, energy, and money (with the right attitude), teaches us to love.

2. It is ok to complain to God and express our problems. But it is not ok to complain against God. Today, go to your Abba (papa), Father and tell Him what is frustrating or broken in your life.

3. Sometimes lying is a habit that was formed to protect ourselves from abuse. Find safety where you can confess and speak truth quickly. Who is a trusted friend where you could safely confess?

Write a Prayer and ask God to help you to express love to others in your speech. Remember love is patient. Love is kind. 1 Corinthians 13:4

Challenge Journal your toxic feelings and practice releasing them to God. Do not hold onto them or they will become bitter and leak out in your speech and poison others and defile yourself. Do you have any anger or bitterness you need to confess?

Truths
• We are accountable for every idle word. Matthew 12:36
• Our words identify what heart condition needs to be confessed and corrected. Matthew 12:34
• Hiding God's Word in my heart keeps me from going astray. Psalm 119:9,11
• I can't control my tongue, but Christ can. James 3:8; Galatians 2:20

Life Skills
• Discipline my thinking. Phil. 4:8
• Meditate on God's Word. Ps. 1:1-3; 119:9-11
• Learn when to be silent. Eccl. 3:7
• Learn when to speak. Eccl. 3:7
• Heart meditation is pure. Psalm 19:14

Promises
• Blessed Psalm 1:1
• Peace of God Philippians 4:9
• Christ lives in me. Galatians 2:20
• Maturity in thoughts and speech. Phil. 4:8

Answers

1. A proud look, hands that shed innocent blood, a heart that devises wicked plans, feet that run to mischief, false witness, discord among others accompany lying.
2. The fear of the Lord is the secret to hating a forward mouth.
3. We should pray to be righteousness so our speech will be right.
4. The lip of truth shall be established forever, but a lying tongue is only for a moment.
5. Idle chatter leads only to poverty (penury).
6. Ungodly people are like a burning fire (out of control forest fire).
7. A lying tongue hates those it lies to.
8. David, the writer of the psalms, is complaining to God.
9. God says that He would sustain us if we cast our burdens on Him.
10. We can ask God to deliver us from a lying tongue.
11. A violent person has poison in their tongue.
12. David prays that the wicked doesn't prosper and that they be taken in their own words and in a deep pit.
13. (Change our hearts) Pray to put off the old man, be renewed in the spirit of your mind, put on the new man, be like God (Christ-like). Pray for righteousness with true holiness.
14. Healthy speech lifts others up and doesn't tear them down.
15. No, followers of God do not speak this way.
16. We can correct our speech by giving thanks.
17. A poisonous tongue is like an uncontrolled fire.
18. Our tongue can defile our entire body.

May you have healthy words that lift others up.

Lesson 11

Taming the Tongue

Do all things without murmurings(complaining) and disputing (arguing). Philippians 2:14

Murmuring-grumbling and complaining

1. Does the Lord want us to blurt out what is on our mind? Proverbs 15:28

2. We can tell that we love ourselves most and hate the person we are speaking with if we do what? Proverbs 16:28

3. If a person blunders and makes a mistake, who do we need to tell? Proverbs 17:9

4. What happens to a person with a forward heart and perverse tongue? Proverbs 17:20

5. What can snare our soul? Proverbs 18:7

6. Should we be honest even if it costs us lots of money? Proverbs 19:1

7. How can we have harmony and healthy relationships with others? Proverbs 26:20-22

8. Burning lips and a wicked heart are pictured as what? Proverbs 26:23

9. When a person hates others, they do what to cover it up? Proverbs 26:24-28

10. How can you tell a man isn't faithful or godly? Psalm 12:1-2

11. What will the Lord do to one with flattering lips or a tongue that speaks proud things? Psalms 12:3

12. How can we dwell (abide) with God in His holy Hill and have a promise to never be moved? Psalm 15

13. What can we do to desire life and have many days? Psalms 34:13

14. How do we keep our tongue from evil and guile (lies)? Psalm 34:9,14

15. A deceitful tongue loves what? Psalm 52:4

16. What may happen to us if we love devouring words? Psalms 52:5

17. David connects what character flaw to the sins of our mouth? Psalm 59:12

18. What battle plan does Paul give us to fight our flesh? Romans 13:10-14

19. Do all things without what? Philippians 2:14
    If we do this what is are blessing in verse 15?

20. What can we do to inherit a blessing when others speak evil of us? I Peter 3:9

Principles
Complaining and arguing is immaturity.

Memory Verse

Do all things without murmurings(complaining) and disputing (arguing). Philippians 2:14

Application
1. He that covers a transgression/sin seeks love. Remember love is part of our armor to fight sin in Romans 13:8-10.

2. Consider going to your offender first if they have a humble heart and are approachable. *If your brother (sister) shall trespass (sin) against you, go and tell them their fault between you and them alone. If they should hear you, you have gained a brother. Matthew 18:15*

3. Great treasures come from seeking God, wisdom, understanding, length of days, and these come when we set our hearts to seek the Lord. It will feel so foreign at first and maybe even worthless use of time, but I promise if you seek Him, you will find Him. This takes intentionality. How could you set our hearts to seek the Lord for the rest of our lives?

Write a Prayer and ask the Lord for a heart to go back and apologize and correct your own speech. Ask to be able to discern your heart motive or wound and why you might over react and respond with harshness.

Challenge If you are fussy to a store clerk or a waiter/waitress, go back and humble yourself and apologize. Make your commitment here to do this:

Do's	Do Not
Think before you answer.	Don't blurt out an answer.
Cover transgression with love.	Don't sow strife.
Walk uprightly.	Don't gossip and slander.
Work righteousness.	Don't repeat a problem.
Speak truth in your heart.	Don't listen to talebearers.
Speak blessings over those who do you wrong.	Don't back-bite.
	Don't do evil (reproach)
	Don't receive an offense against your neighbor.
	Don't render evil for evil.
	Don't rail if you are railed.

Consequences for Unruly Speech
• Cut off
• Destroyed
• Rooted out of the land
• Falls into mischief
• Falls into no good
• Considered a fool
• Will bring their own destruction
• Will ruin their own soul.

Blessing
• Never be moved
• Abide (dwell) with God
• We will shine as lights in the world.

Wrong Heart Motives
Fair speech, flattery, deceit, to work ruin, selfish gain

Answers

1.No, the Lord doesn't want us to blurt out answers but to study what we will say.

2.If we sow strife (arguments/back-stabbing) or gossip, we are considered forward (perverse).

3.If we are seeking love, we will cover the transgression. If we repeat the matter to others, we could be separating good friends.

4.A person with a perverse or forward tongue falls into mischief and no good.

5.A fool's mouth is their destruction and traps their soul.

6.Yes, it is better to be poor with integrity (honesty) than to be one with perverse (stubborn) lips.

7.Avoid being a talebearer and don't listen to one. Talebearing causes wounds to others. Don't be around those who are contentious.

8.Potsherd is charcoal covered with silver, it is cheap. Godly lips are pure silver. Dross is the impurities that come from silver.

9.A wicked person will disguise their hatred with their lips and be deceitful even though their speech is nice. Their hatred is exposed as they roll into the pit, they dug for another. Their mouth works ruin.

10.Ungodly person speaks vanity (mean empty things), flattering lips, double heart/deception (which means they aren't consistent in their speech or actions).

11.The Lord will cut off someone with ungodly speech.

12.A. Walk uprightly

B. Work righteousness.

C. Speak truth (don't lie to yourself or others)

D. Don't backbite with your tongue

E. Don't do evil (mischief) to your neighbor.

F. Don't take up offense with your neighbor.

G. Despise a vile person.

H. Honor those that fear the Lord.

I. Keep your promises (change not) or do make conditions to your words… for example, if it doesn't rain, we will or if nothing else comes up we will, etc.

J. Don't loan money for interest. (I think it is speaking about to your godly brother.)

K. Don't take a reward against the innocent.

13. Keep our tongue from evil and our lips from speaking guile (lies).

14. We are to fear (respect) the Lord, seek the Lord, listen, (hearken) to the Lord, depart from evil, seek peace.

15. A deceitful tongue loves devouring words (gossip, slander, rude, breaking the spirit words).

16. God may destroy forever & pluck us out of our dwelling place and root us out of the land of the living.

17. David connects the sin of our mouth with pride.

18. A. Love one another. Awake out of a spiritual slumber/sleep,
B. Put on the armor of light (by doing right),
C. walk honestly,
D. make no provisions for the flesh to fulfill the lust thereof. Example: Stay away from places, people, situations that draw you away from God or tempt you to sin. Set up good boundaries for ourselves.
19. Instruction is to do all things without murmurings (complaining) and disputing (arguing)
The blessing is that "We will shine as lights in the world.
20.Don't render evil for evil, railing for railing, but speak a blessing. (This is what we are called for and we will inherit a blessing.)

Blessing

I bless each one of you with a wholesome tongue. A tongue ruled by kindness and gentleness. A tongue that speaks no evil, never lies and quickly repents and forgives others. A tongue ruled by love. I ask the Lord to help you choose your words carefully and help you to have a controlled tongue that can be quiet. May your words be encouraging and uplifting others. May they be like sweet honey and a refreshing breeze. May each one of you refuse to complain or argue but turn your complaint into thankfulness and your arguing into problem solving solutions. May you today and forever from this day forward choose to praise and glorify God with your words. Amen

Lesson 12

Treasures

For where your treasure is, there your heart will be also.
Matthew 6:21

Treasure-something very much valued.

1. Proverbs 16:8 Would it be ok to do wrong if you will get wealth/financial gain for it?

2. Proverbs 16:16 What is better than gold? What is better than silver?

3. Proverbs 17:1 Compare the difference between a quiet or strifeful home?

4. Ecclesiastes 5:10 What is the problem is this verse?

5. Ecclesiastes 5:15 Did a person bring riches when they were born? Can he take it with him when he dies?

6. Ecclesiastes 5:19-20 What is our gift?

7. Matthew 6:19 What is the instruction in this verse?

8. Matthew 6:20 So where should your treasure be?

9. Matthew 6:21 Where is your heart?

10. Matthew 6:24 Can you serve two masters?

11. 1 Corinthians 2:9 What kind of things does the Lord have stored for us?

12. Psalm 119:11 What treasure is a young person to hide in their heart?

13. 1 Kings 3:7-9 What was Solomon's request?

14. 1 Kings 3:10 Was Solomon's request pleasing to the Lord?

15. I Kings 3:12-13 What kind of heart did God give Solomon and what else did God give him?

16. I Kings 3:14 What was the condition Solomon had to meet to also receive "length of days"?

17. I Kings 3:15, What was Solomon's first response when he awoke from his dream?

Principles
Your actions will reveal the treasures of your heart.

Memory Verse
For where your treasure is, there will your heart be also. Matthew 6:21

Application
1. Rehearse a Scripture before you go to bed and if you awake at night troubled, remember to take long deep breaths and rehearse your verse. *It is vain for you to rise up early, to sit up late, to eat the bread of sorrows; for so He gives His beloved sleep. Psalm 127:2*

2. Whatever I focus on will grow. What do you focus on?

3. If you want to give others these secret heavenly treasures, it must be done with sweetness, or they cannot receive it. *The wise in heart shall be called prudent, and sweetness of the lips increases learning. Proverbs 16:21*

Write a Prayer and ask God for the great treasure of wisdom and understanding to make right decisions.

Challenge Be mindful today of what you think about in your passive thoughts. If you are troubled, shift your focus from problems to praising God. Write a problem and then find some small thing to be grateful about in the circumstance?

Truths
• Money is a gift from God to provide for you.
• Be content with your station in life.

• Store treasures in heaven.
• It all belongs to God.
• Unimaginable treasures in Christ.

Precepts

• Wealth never satisfies.
    o   Wealth gives us worries.
    o   Wealth robs us of our sleep.

• We brought nothing in this world and can take nothing with us when we die.

Better than
• Wisdom is better than gold.
• Understanding is better than silver.
• Better is little with quietness than wealth with strife.

Answers

1. A righteous person would not compromise their standards but would act in a way to show love and obedience to God.

2. Wisdom is better than gold, Understanding is to be chose over silver.

3. Better to have little with quietness, than a house full of feasting with strife.

4. Those that love money will only want more money; they will never be satisfied or have enough. This misplaced affection will cause problems with money: and give us too many things to worry you and robs us of our sleep.

5. No, we brought nothing into this world. We can take nothing with us when we die.

6. The Lord gives us money as a gift to enjoy our lives with as much or as little as He gives us. When we are satisfied with our lot in life our focus will be on joy.

7. Lay not up treasures on earth because moth and rust destroy it or where thieves will steal our treasures on earth.

8. My treasures are to be stored in heaven.

9. The treasures of heaven are love, joy, peace, courage, faith, and the things money cannot buy.

10. No, I cannot serve two masters. Hint: Whatever I think of most is my master. Even my fear or worries can master me.

11. The Lord has stored many unimaginable treasures for us.

12. God's Word is a treasure to be hidden in our heart. This treasure can never be stolen. It will never rot, rust and moths cannot eat it. And it will guide us all our life.

13. Solomon requested an understanding heart and to be able to judge between good and evil.

14. Yes, God was pleased when Solomon asked for wisdom and not riches or power.

15. God gave Solomon a wise and understanding heart and added great riches and honor.

16. Solomon was instructed to walk in God's ways, keep God's statutes and commandments.

17. Solomon's first response was to go and worship God.

May you store your treasures in heaven.

Lesson 13

Finding Reward

And whatsoever you do, do it heartily, as to the Lord, and not unto men...(and) you shall receive the reward of the inheritance.
Colossian 3:23-24

Revive (convert)- means to return the consciousness of life (soul), restore or renew.

1. Psalm 19:7a What two things can God's perfect law (Scriptures) do for me?

2. Psalm 19:8 What are statutes?

3. Psalm 19:8a How will I know if God's statutes have taken hold of my life?

4. Psalm 19:8b-9a How can the commandment enlighten the eyes?

5. Psalm 19:9 What will endure forever?
Is there anything in the Word of God that isn't righteous?

6. Psalm 19:10 When we seek God's presence in His Word how does the psalmist describe it?

7. Psalm 19:11 What are the two blessings in this verse?

8. Psalm 19:12 Can I discern my errors, and can I be cleansed from my secret faults?

9. Psalm 19:13a What are willful/presumptuous sins? What does it mean that sin may have dominion over me?

10. Psalm 19:14a What should be our heart cry?

11. Psalm 19:14b Who is our strength and our redeemer?

12. Hebrews 10:35 So what character trait do we need to persevere to receive the reward?

13. Hebrews 11:6 What do we need to earnestly practice?

14. 2 John 1:7-8 What should I guard myself against?

15. Colossians 3:23-24 Who am I serving?

Principles
God rewards those who serve Him.

Memory Verses

And whatsoever you do, do it heartily, as to the Lord, and not unto men…(and) you shall receive the reward of the inheritance. Colossian 3:23-24

Application

1. Great reward comes with diligently seeking His presence in the Word. When you seek the Lord can you find His felt presence of peace?

2. Our mouths will reflect our hearts. Listen to your complaints and you will how where you need healing. *For out of the abundance of the heart the mouth speaks. Matthew 12:34*

3. If you are trapped in a sinful behavior and cannot stop. Find a few deliverance Scriptures in the Psalms and pray them earnestly until you are set free.

Write a Prayer and ask God to help you love His Word that you may be made wise and warned of evil. Without being rooted and grounded in the pure, clean, enlightening and enduring Word of God we will be easily deceived and led astray. *O taste and see that the Lord is good; blessed is the man that trust in Him! Psalm 34:8*

Challenge Meditate on a verse from Scripture until it becomes sweeter than honey and more precious than gold. Something as simple as *"the Lord is my Shepherd"* can reset your affections on the Lord all day. *Set your affection on things above, not on things on the earth. Colossians 3:2*

Law (Word)

- Revives the soul.
- Makes the simple wise.
- Converts foolish person to wise.
- It teaches statutes which are boundaries and safety nets to make decisions and protect us.
- More precious than gold.
- Sweeter than honey.

Commandments

- Enlightens the eyes.
- Rejoices the heart.
- Warns of evil.
- Gives great reward.
- Reveals my secret faults.

Lord's Work

- Deliverer
- Strength
- Redeemer

My Work with the Holy Spirit's Help

- Develop confidence in God.
- Persevere until the end.
- Serve others like I am serving God and not man.
- Guard against deceivers.
- Speak wholesome words.
- Meditate on wholesome thoughts.

Answers

1. Yes, the law is perfect. The law can revive my soul. The law can make the simple wise.
2. Statutes are standards from God's Word. They are like boundaries or safety nets.
3. I will be rejoicing and trusting God even in great difficulties.
4. The commandments can enlighten the eyes because they are so pure and transparent, we can see clearly now.
5. The fear (reverence) of the Lord will endure forever. The Word of God is altogether righteous.
6. The Word is more precious than gold, than much pure gold. The Word is sweeter than honey from the comb.
7. The first blessing is that I am warned of evil. The second is that I will receive great reward.
8. I can pray to understand my secret faults and ask for forgiveness.
9. Sins that we willingly commit, even when we know they are sins are presumptuous. For sin to have dominion over me, means that I could be trapped in a sin and unable to escape without God's deliverance.
10. May the words of my mouth and the meditation of my heart be pleasing in Your sight.
11. The Lord is our strength and redeemer.
12. We need confidence to continue in the will of God so we may receive our reward in the end.
13. We must practice faith and believe that our faith will lead to our reward.
14. I must guard myself against deceivers that will try to rob me of my faith in Jesus Christ.
15. I am serving the Lord, Jesus Christ and am to work for Him with all my heart and not working for men.

May the Lord be your strength and redeemer.

Lesson 14

Who am I?

But as many as received him, to them he gave power to become the children of God, even to them that believe on his name. John 1:12

Redeemed-ransomed, delivered from bondage, distress, penalty, liability, or from the possession of another.

As Christians, we are bought for a price. We are redeemed from slavery and belong to Christ. We are free in Christ. *For he that is called in the Lord... is the Lord's freeman... You are bought with a price ... therein abide with God. 1 Corinthians 7:22-24*

1. John 1:12 Who am I?

2. John 15:15 Who am I to Christ?

3. Romans 5:1 How can we be reconciled (justified) with God?

4. 1 Corinthians 6:17 Who does God want me to unite (join) with and why?

5. Ephesians 1:1 How does Paul address believers?

6. Ephesians 1:5 How can we become saints?

7. Ephesians 2:13 Can we have assurance of salvation?

8. Colossians 1:14 Do I have to carry my guilt anymore?

9. Colossians 2:10 What have I been given in Christ?

Principle
I am a child of God.

Memory Verse

But as many as received him, to them he gave power to become the children of God, even to them that believe on his name.

John 1:12

Application
1. According to our memory verse the only thing we need to do is receive Him and believe in His name. *Yet to all who did receive him, to those who believed in his name, he gave the right to become children of God— children born not of natural descent, nor of human decision or a husband's will, but born of God. John 1:13* Have you received Jesus Christ as your Savior?

2. Today, I pray for you to be filled with the knowledge of His will in all wisdom and spiritual understanding. ...*(we) do not cease to pray for you, and to desire that you might be filled with the knowledge of his will in all wisdom and spiritual understanding. Colossians 1:9* Pray for the Holy Spirit that you may be empowered to have the desire to be filled with His knowledge, wisdom and spiritual understanding.

3. When we give ourselves to the Lord, it is our inheritance to have Christ's righteousness and the felt presence of peace and joy. We no longer need to believe the lie that we are orphans or don't have a Father to go to in time of need. We have safely trust in God to be our comforter, provider and protector. Ask God for the reality of His kingdom in your life. *The kingdom of God is not meat and drink, but righteousness, and peace, and joy in the Holy Ghost.*

Write a Prayer and ask God to deliver you from the power of darkness and transfer you into the kingdom of Christ, Jesus. *Who (God) has delivered us from the power of darkness and has translated us into the kingdom of his dear Son. Colossians 1:13*

Challenge Today meet every challenging circumstance with *all patience and longsuffering with joyfulness. Colossians 1:11* This is an intentional practice of embracing the kingdom of God which is your inheritance as His child. This takes mature faith and *to be strengthened with all might according to his glorious power... Colossian 1:11*

Child of God
• Adjoined to Christ. 1 Corinthians 6:12
• Joined in one Spirit. 1 Corinthians 6:17
• Filled with all knowledge and understanding. Colossians 1:9
• Partakers of inheritance of the saints of light. Colossians 1:12
• Delivered from darkness and translated into the kingdom of God. Colossians 1:13
• Redeemed through the blood of Jesus with forgiveness of sins. Colossians 1:14

Truths	Promises
• We are justified through faith. • We are saints. • We are adopted as sons & daughters through Christ. • We are brought near by the blood of Christ. • We have fullness and completeness in Christ.	• We are children of God. *If we receive Him. • He will make known to us the things of the Father.

Answers

1) If I receive Jesus, this is the power to become a child of God.

2) I am Jesus's friend. The promise is that He will make known to me the things from the Father.

3) We are justified by faith through the Lord Jesus Christ. Pray for this gift of faith.

4) I am to adjoin with Christ Jesus Lord, then I will be one spirit with Him. 1 Corinthians 6:12 indicates that this adjoining our self with Christ will empower us to not be mastered, overpowered or controlled by anything.

5) Paul addresses believers as saints and faithful in Christ Jesus.

6) It is for God's pleasure that He adopts us into His family through Jesus Christ, His Son.

7) Yes, we are sealed with the Holy Spirit of promise.

8) No, in Christ Jesus we have redemption and forgiveness of sins. Read Colossians 1:12-13 for more confidence.

9) I have been given the fullness (completeness) in Christ. Jesus Christ is head over every power and authority.

May you be adjoined to Christ in one Spirit.

Lesson 15
Salvation Pathway

For by grace are you saved through faith; and that not our yourselves: it is the gift of God. Ephesians 2:8

Grace-free and unmerited favor that we do not deserve. Favor; mercy; pardon.

1. John 3:16 What is our responsibility?

2. Romans 3:23 Why do we need a Savior?

3. Romans 6:23 If we turn from our sin, what is the promise?

4. Romans 10:9 What is my resposibility?

5. Romans 10:13 How can I be saved?

6. Romans 10:17 How can I increase my faith?

7. Revelation 3:20 Who wants to come into our lives and fellowship with us?

8. Ephesians 2:8 How are we saved?

Principle
Salvation is a gift from God.

Memory Verse

For by grace are you saved through faith; and
that not our yourselves: it is the gift of God.
Ephesians 2:8

Application

1. There is a sorrow that leads to repentance. We need to know our own depravity and need for a Savior. Peter fully repented for his denial of Jesus and then fed the sheep. *And Peter went out and wept bitterly. Luke 22:62" "Simon, son of John, do you love me more than these?" "Yes, Lord," he said, "you know that I love you." Jesus said, "Feed my lambs." John 21:15*

2. There is a sorrow that leads to sorrow and self-destruction. *5 And he (Judas) cast down the pieces of silver in the temple and departed, and went and hanged himself. Matthew 27 I pray that your sorrow will lead to repentance and not despair.*

3. There is a fight to hold onto your faith and continue to have a clear conscience. Many will scoff or mock our love for Christ, and we will be tempted to tone it down or to try to fit in with the world. But instead develop thick skin and burn strong for Jesus. ...*wage a good warfare, holding faith and a good conscience which some, having put aside, have suffered shipwreck concerning faith. 1 Timothy 1:19* Ask the Lord to forgive your persecutors.

Write a Prayer ask God to do a good work in you. *Being confident of this very thing, that He who has begun a good work in you will perform it until the Day of Jesus Christ. Philippians 1:6*

Challenge Forgive yourself. What regret do you need to let go? Wrtie one kind thing to yourself here.

Answers

1. Our responsibility is to believe.
2. We have all sinned and fallen short of the glory of God.
3. The gift of God is eternal life through Jesus Christ our Lord.
4. To confess with our mouth and believe in our heart is our responsibility.
5. Call upon the name of the Lord.
6. Faith comes by hearing the Word of God. Listen for God's voice.
7. Jesus stands at the door and knocks at the door of our hearts.
8. For by grace are you saved through faith, it is a gift of God.

May you receive the grace of God for enduring faith.

LEADERSHIP GUIDELINES

Dishonorable Leadership	Honorable Leadership
Anger	Happy Countenance
Use of fear tactics	Approachable
Threats/Bullying	Patient and Kind
Retaliation for being confronted	Gracious; holds others accountable
Hasty/Rash	Treats everyone the same
Impatient	Good self-identity
Arrogant	Good boundaries
Values self, money, or project goals more than others	Good mentors Good relationships
Holds a grudge	Unemotional decision maker
Plays favorites	Leads through serving
Casts confusion on situations to blame shift	Humble- Leads with power and under submission to their authority
Makes emotional decisions not principally based decisions	Will do what is right, no matter the consequences
Denies problems	Good listener
Deals only with superficial problems	Forgives easily, coaches weaker ones; encourages others.
Ignores the main problem	Identifies root problems
Does not seek counsel	Seek many counselors
Ask impossible things	Able to plan and develop goals
Unrealistic/Demanding	Able to follow through with a plan
*Adapted from observation of the behaviors of Daniel and Nebuchadnezzar the pagan king in the book of Daniel.	Always same level of emotional availability

Rules: No bullying or verbal abuse ever!
Kind, patient but sometimes very firm!

GOOD FOLLOWER

1. Respects Authority
2. Protects Good Name
3. Learns to Stand Alone (not follow a crowd)
4. Guards the truth
5. Takes responsibility for actions
6. Honorable and fair in decisions
7. Makes good sound financial decisions
8. Lives with Self-Control
9. Moderation in all things
10. Gives good days work without complaint
11. Always on time; dependable
12. Never gossips, slanders, or accuses
13. Takes any issues up the ladder through the chain of command
14. Guards all that is entrusted into their hands; trustworthy
15. Refuses to do anything illegal, unethical, or immoral

*You must learn to be a good follower to be a good leader.

AUTHOR'S BIOGRAPHIES

Angie G. Meadows graduated from St Mary's School of Nursing as a Registered Nurse, Marshall University with a bachelor's in nursing and Ohio State University with a master's in nursing. Angie is an ordained minister. She is currently a mother, grandmother, speaker, and writer. Her favorite pastime is quilting and mentoring those in active recovery from substance use disorder. Angie is currently, recording podcasts, radio shows and building programs to mentor and disciple others in Christ to grow and mature others in their Christian walk.

www.ingramcontent.com/pod-product-compliance
Lightning Source LLC
Chambersburg PA
CBHW060328050426
42449CB00011B/2702